MY SPORT
NETBALL

Tim Wood

Photographs: Chris Fairclough

Franklin Watts
London • New York • Sydney • Toronto

Franklin Watts
96 Leonard Street
London EC2A 4RH

Phototypeset by Lineage, Watford
Printed in Italy
by G. Canale, Turin

Design by: K & Co

UK ISBN: 0 74960 132 9

Illustrations: Simon Roulestone, Aziz Khan

Photographs on pages 27, 28 and 29 by Richard
Sharpley

The publishers, author and photographer would
like to thank Joanne and Michelle Hall, Mrs Hall,
Kathleen Edwards, the Headmaster of New
Wellington High School, Altrincham, Liz
Broomhead and Liz Nicholl for their help and
co-operation in the production of this book.

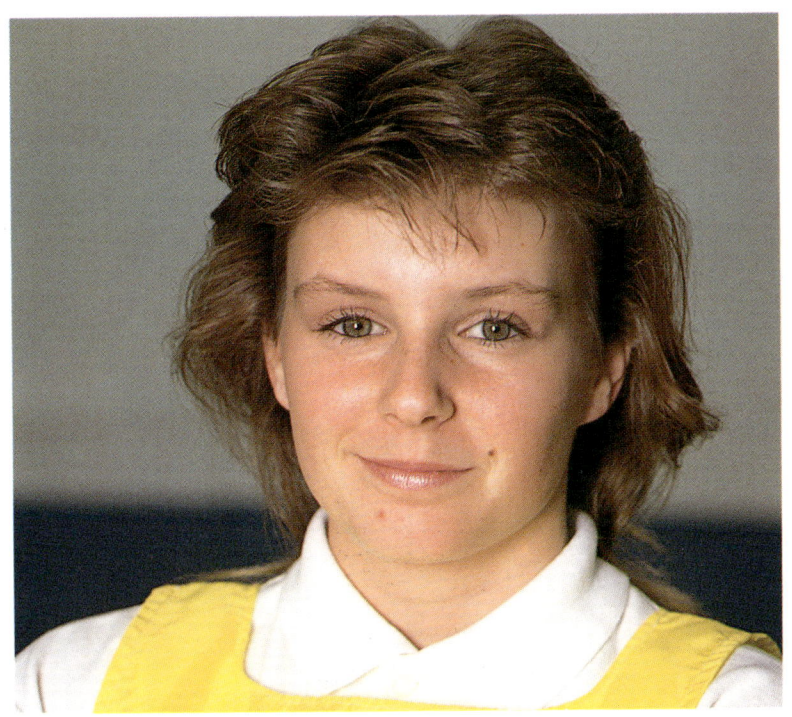

The netball player featured in this book is Joanne Hall. Joanne is seventeen years old. She started playing netball at her primary school. At the age of fifteen she played for her school netball team. The team won the National Schools Under 16 Netball Championships, and shortly afterwards Joanne was asked to attend an England Schoolgirl trial. She failed to make the team on that occasion, but was selected the following year. Since then she has played for the Greater Manchester County team, the Northwest Region under 21s, the All England Under 18s and also the Young England Under 21s. Joanne likes netball because she enjoys playing team games, keeping fit and travelling.

I am a netball player. I usually start my training sessions with a run. This helps me to build up my stamina so my body can stand up to the fast and furious action on the netball court.

4

Back in the gym, I do some fast skipping. This is not only good for my heart and legs, but also helps me to be light on my feet. Agility is an important skill for top netball players.

5

I do some leg exercises to stretch my hamstrings. Warming up my hamstrings and leg muscles properly helps me to avoid injury in a game.

I play Goal Shooter so it is most important for me to have a powerful shot. Working out on the multi-gym helps me to improve my arm strength.

I want to use the ball for the final stages of my fitness training. First, I have to pump it up to the correct pressure. A match ball should weigh about 425g (15oz). This one is made of rubber.

I use the ball for some more stretching exercises.
This one develops suppleness in my back and
helps improve my fingertip control of the ball.

Once my fitness training is over, I start to work on my skills. It is vital when under pressure in a match, to be able to catch and pass the ball with either hand. Tossing it from hand to hand helps me to develop ambidexterity.

My twin sister is also a county netball player. She trains with me. Tossing two balls to each other at high speed helps both of us to improve our handling and ball control.

My most important job in the team is to score goals. It is hardest to score from a position directly in front of the goal-post, so I practise this shot at least fifty times each day.

As I shoot, I 'snap' my wrist to put backspin on the ball. If the ball does not go straight into the net, the backspin will help it drop back through the ring.

MORE ABOUT NETBALL

There are seven players in a netball team.

Netball is a fast-moving and exciting game to play. The aim of the game is to pass the ball up the court, making sure it is played in each third, and to score a goal.

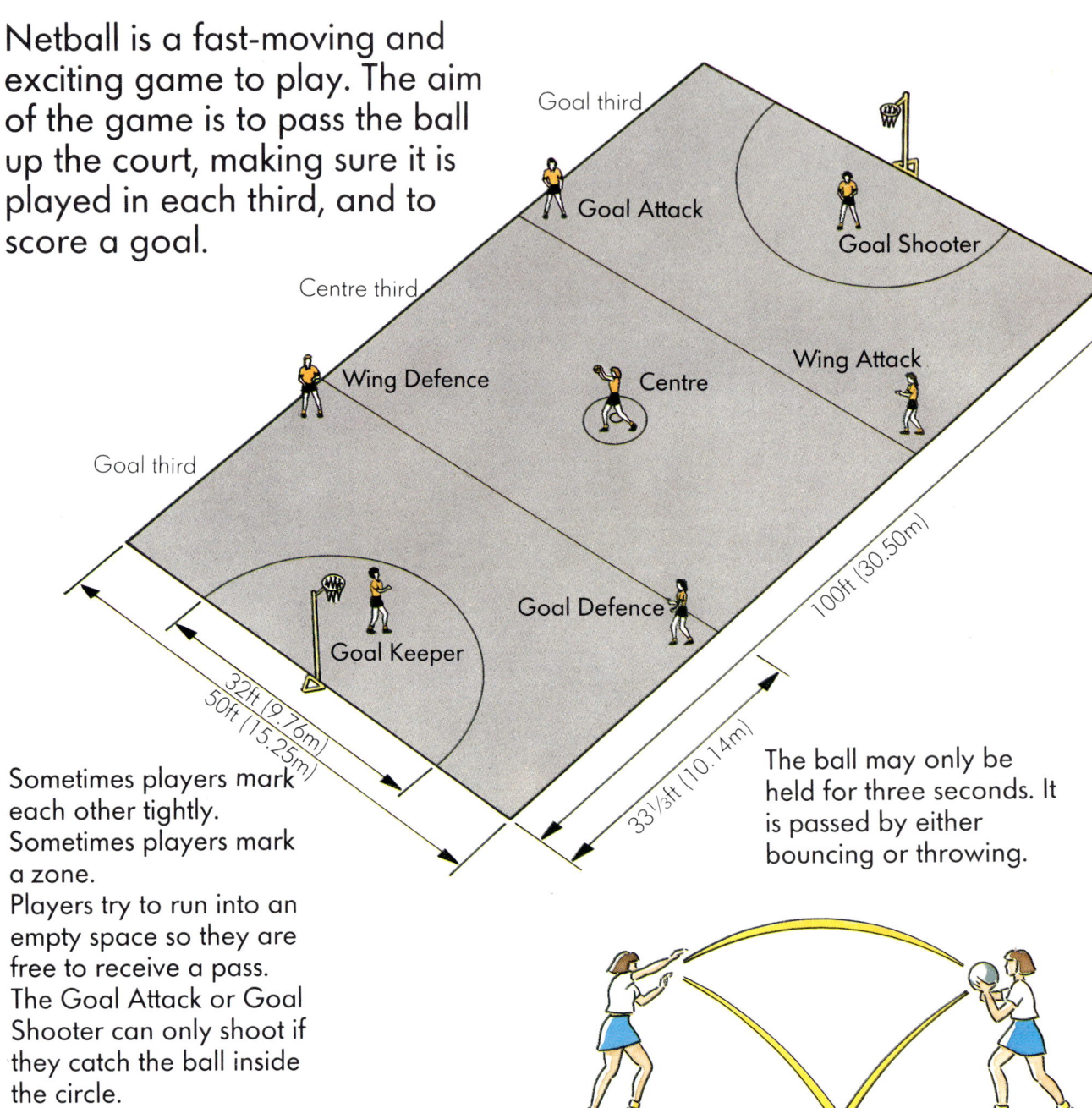

Goal third

Goal Attack

Goal Shooter

Centre third

Wing Defence

Centre

Wing Attack

Goal third

Goal Defence

Goal Keeper

32ft (9.76m)

50ft (15.25m)

33⅓ft (10.14m)

100ft (30.50m)

Sometimes players mark each other tightly.
Sometimes players mark a zone.
Players try to run into an empty space so they are free to receive a pass.
The Goal Attack or Goal Shooter can only shoot if they catch the ball inside the circle.

The ball may only be held for three seconds. It is passed by either bouncing or throwing.

14

A netball court is divided into five areas. Each player can only play in her own area.

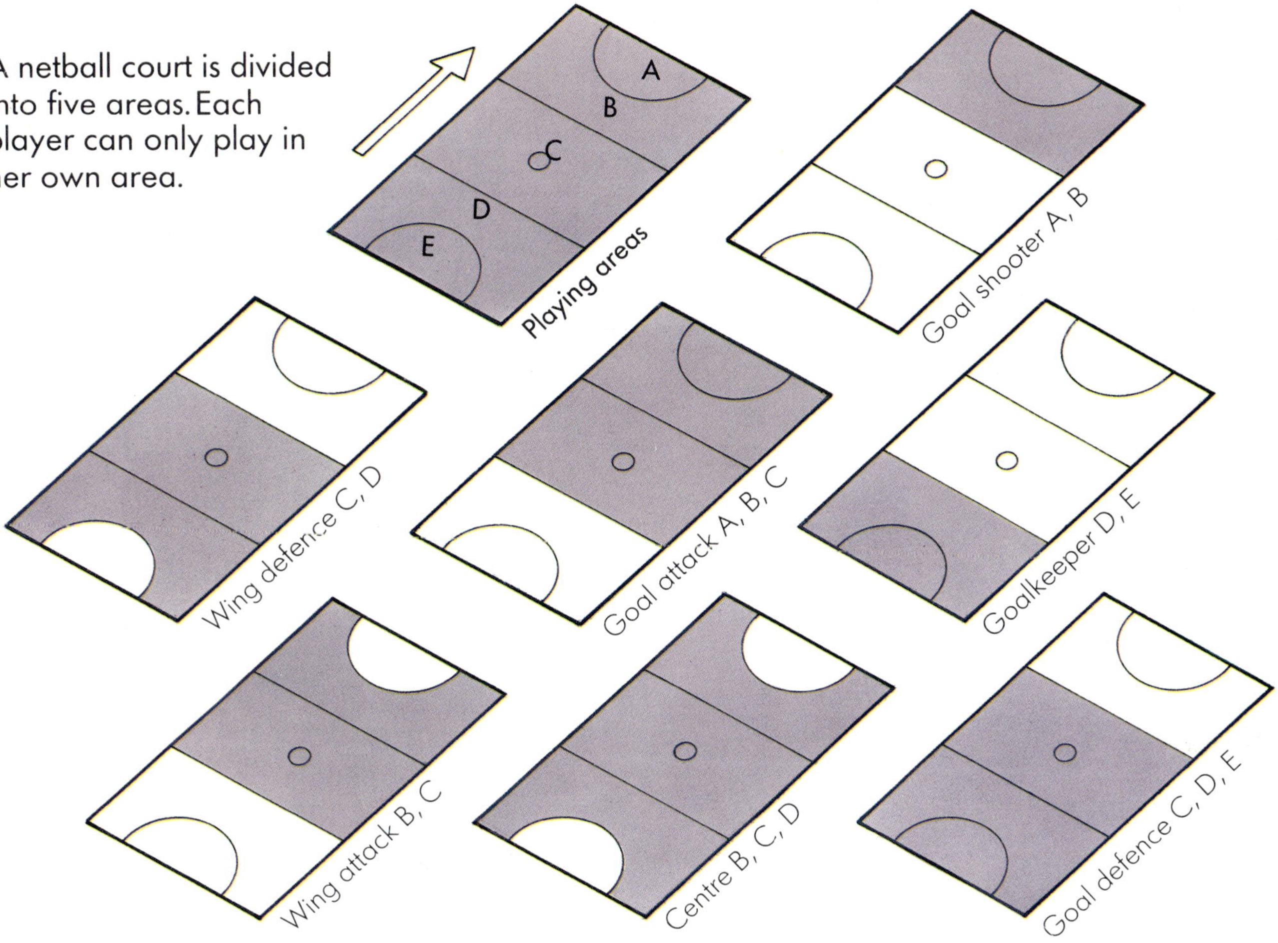

Playing areas

A
B
C
D
E

Goal shooter A, B

Wing defence C, D

Goal attack A, B, C

Goalkeeper D, E

Wing attack B, C

Centre B, C, D

Goal defence C, D, E

Once a player has caught a pass, she may only move the foot that she didn't land on before passing the ball.

A player may pivot on her landing foot and move her other foot in any direction, any number of times.

The throw-up is used to start a game or restart play when possession of the ball is undecided.

15

After we finish our individual training session, we are going on to a county team practice. Our county coach gives us a few words of advice before we leave.

The whole county squad starts the training session on an outside court. We are organised into groups to work on our ball-handling skills. This exercise is designed to improve our passing and catching.

When the practice game starts, I position myself within range of the goal. I have to stay alert, watch the play and be ready to run into a free space to receive a pass.

My sister, who is playing Goal Attack, tries a shot. I position myself ready to catch the ball if she misses the goal. I may be able to catch a rebound and try a shot myself.

During the game, the opposing Goal Keeper marks me closely. She tries to intercept any balls passed to me, and to stop me shooting. I watch for opportunities to get free from her.

Goal Shooters who stay by the goal-post are easy to mark. I get free by making a quick run into open space to receive a pass. I am outside the circle, so I cannot attempt a shot. When I pivot, I will have to pass into the circle.

Fast, accurate passing is one of the main skills needed in netball. I try to pass to where I know the receiver will be in a split second, and not to where she is now. This keeps the attack moving forward at high speed.

If an opponent near me catches the ball, she will pass it to one of her team mates. I try to stop her doing this. I can either reach up to interfere with her throw or, as in this case, jump to intercept her pass.

23

The Goal Keeper tries to defend against my shot. I make myself ignore her movements as I concentrate on my shooting.

It is vital for a Goal Shooter to be able to score from anywhere in the circle. A shot from a position close to the side of the goal is the most straightforward.

I score about eighty per cent of the goals I attempt. I have to practise shooting from every position in the circle in order to keep up my average. This training helps me to score goals even when I am falling over.

I have been called for a trial for the England team. On the morning of the trial I feel nervous, although I hope to regain my place in the squad. The national coach tells us what she expects from us before the game starts.

I am determined to do well. The opposing Goal Keeper is taller than me so I must literally keep on my toes to be faster to the ball! I mark her even more closely than I usually do.

I scored 26 goals during the game and played well enough to be selected for the England squad. I feel very proud. I can look forward to the new season, but I know I must play extra hard to keep my place in the team.

Facts about netball

Rules for netball were first laid down in Britain in 1901.

The first international netball matches took place in 1949 between England, Scotland and Wales.

In 1956, Australia became the first overseas team to visit England. In the same year, an England team toured South Africa.

The first world netball tournament was held in 1963. World tournaments are now held every four years.

The record for being world champions most times is held by Australia. They have won the World Championships five times.

The record for the highest number of international appearances is held by Jillean Hipsey of England. She represented her country 100 times between 1978 and 1987.

Games similar to netball were played in Ancient Greece and Rome. The Roman game had three players on each side.

Modern netball is a direct descendant of American basketball. It developed in America and was first introduced into this country in 1895 by an American, Dr Toles.

Netball was first played at Madame Osterberg's College of Physical training in North London. The young ladies there were taught it as a form of indoor basketball. There were no written rules and no lines on the court. The goals were waste-paper baskets hung on the walls.

GLOSSARY

Agility
The skill of moving quickly and lightly.

Ambidexterity
Being able to use both hands with equal skill

Backspin
A force put on the ball which makes it spin backwards.

Circle
A semi-circular area at each end of a netball court inside which all shooting must take place.

Intercept
To catch a pass meant for a member of the opposing team.

Pivot
To spin round on one or both feet to face in the opposite direction.

Rebound
A ball which bounces off the goal-post.

Snap
To put backspin on to the ball.

Squad
A group of players which trains together and from which the main team is chosen.

Stamina
Staying power.

Third
An area of a netball court which is equal to one third of its area.

Trial
A game or series of games played in order to select a squad.

INDEX